The Hungry Dragon

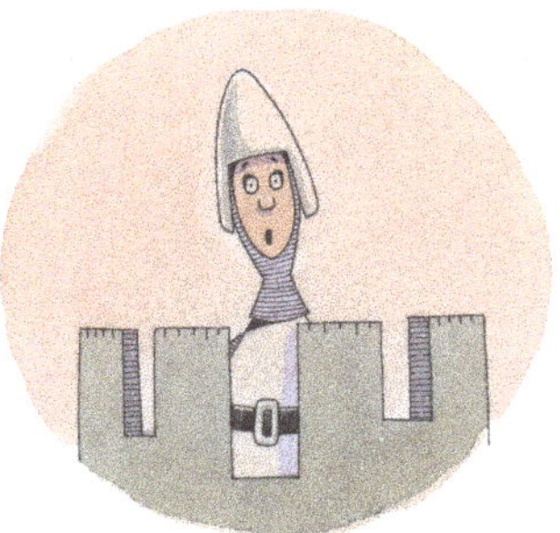

Fay Robinson
Illustrated by Mark Oliver

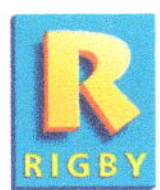

RIGBY

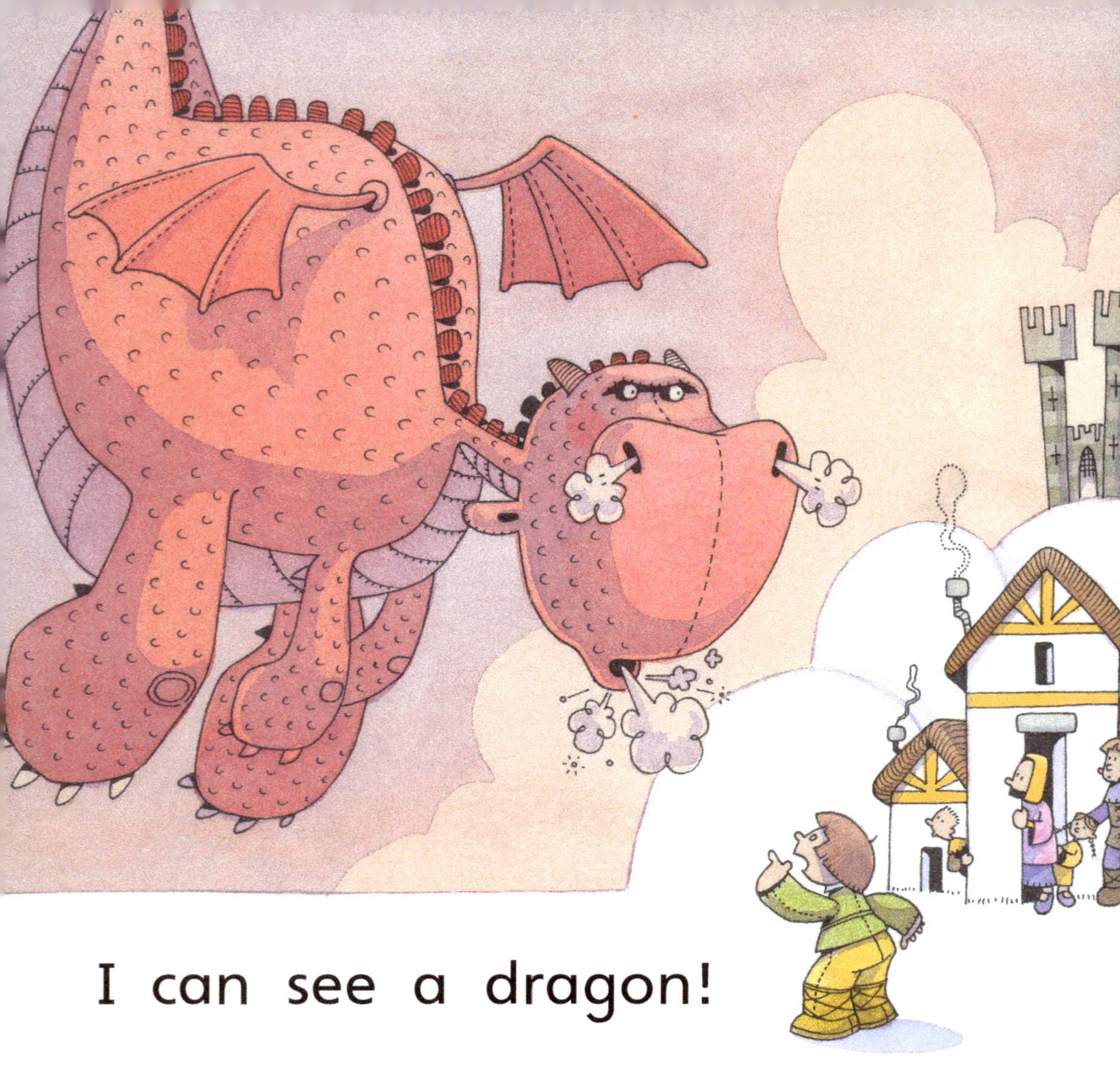

I can see a dragon!

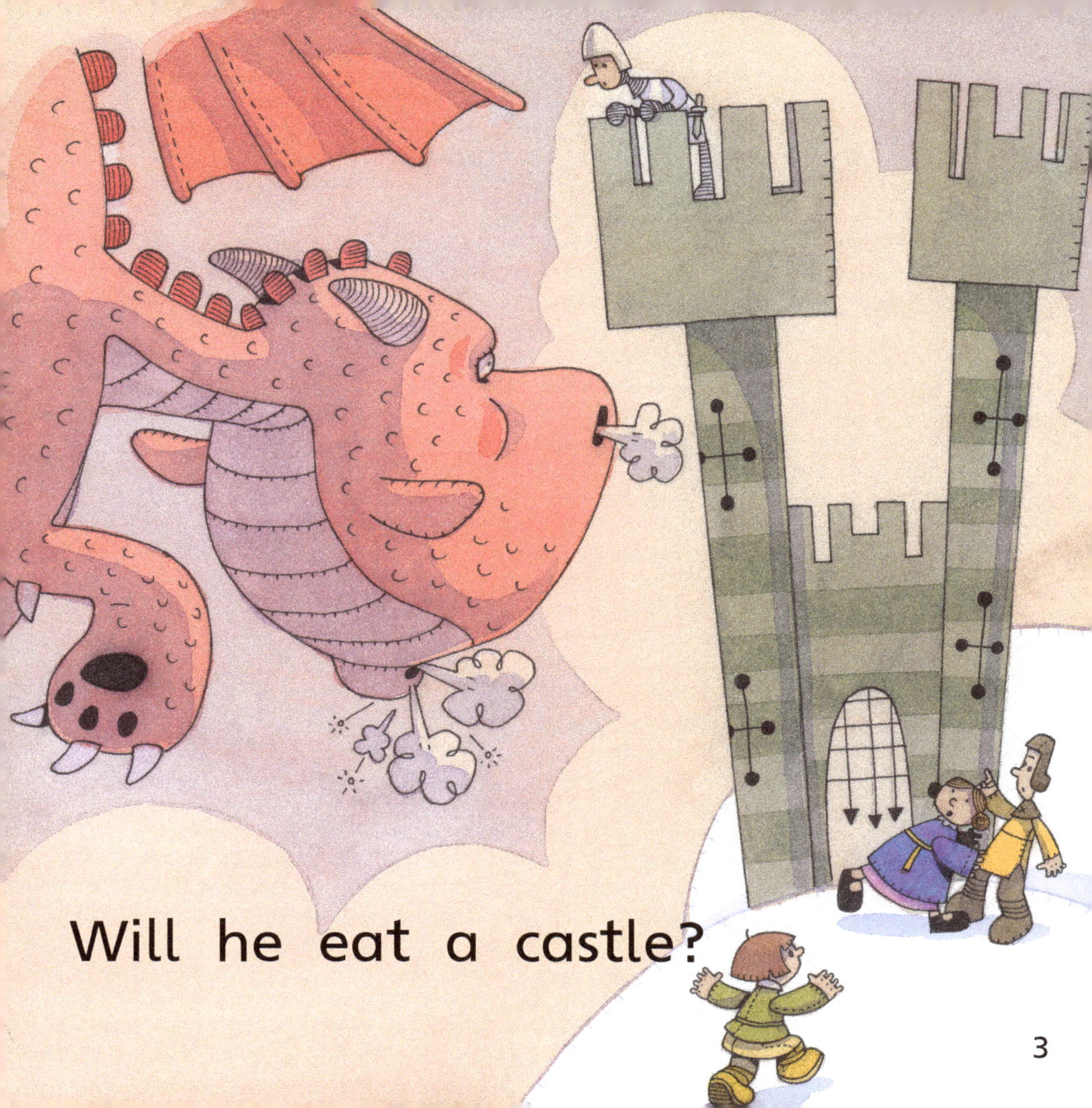

Will he eat a castle?

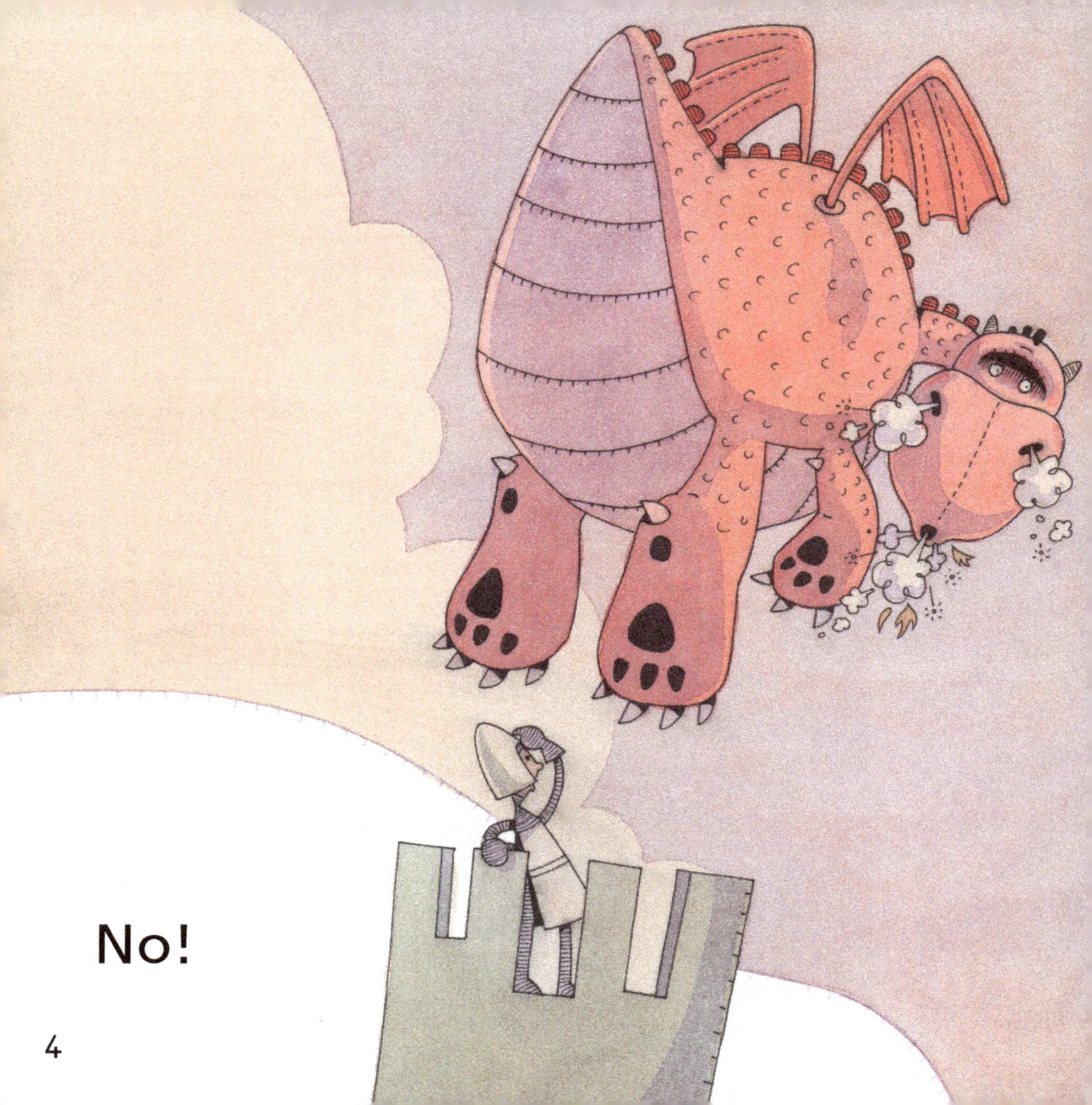

No!

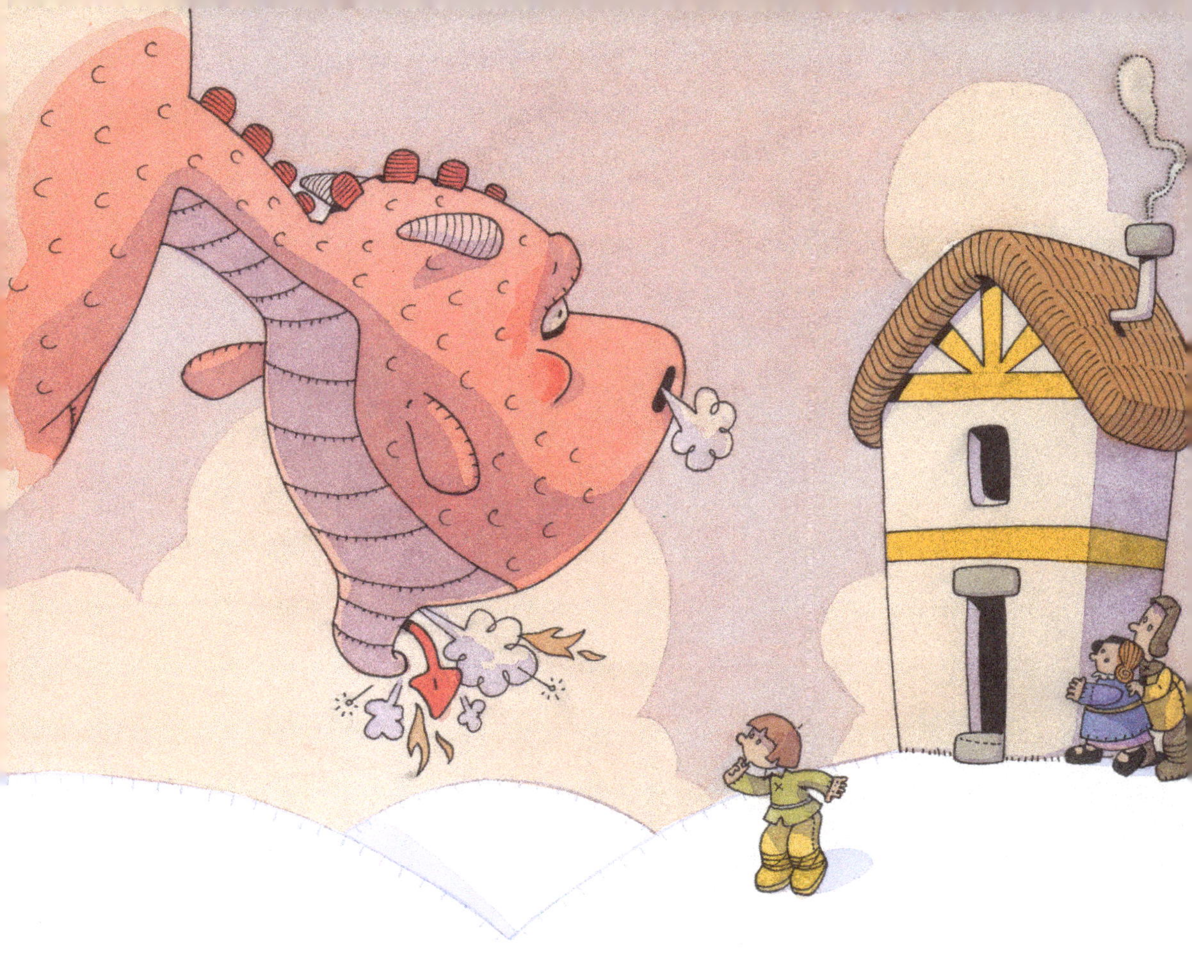

Will he eat a house?

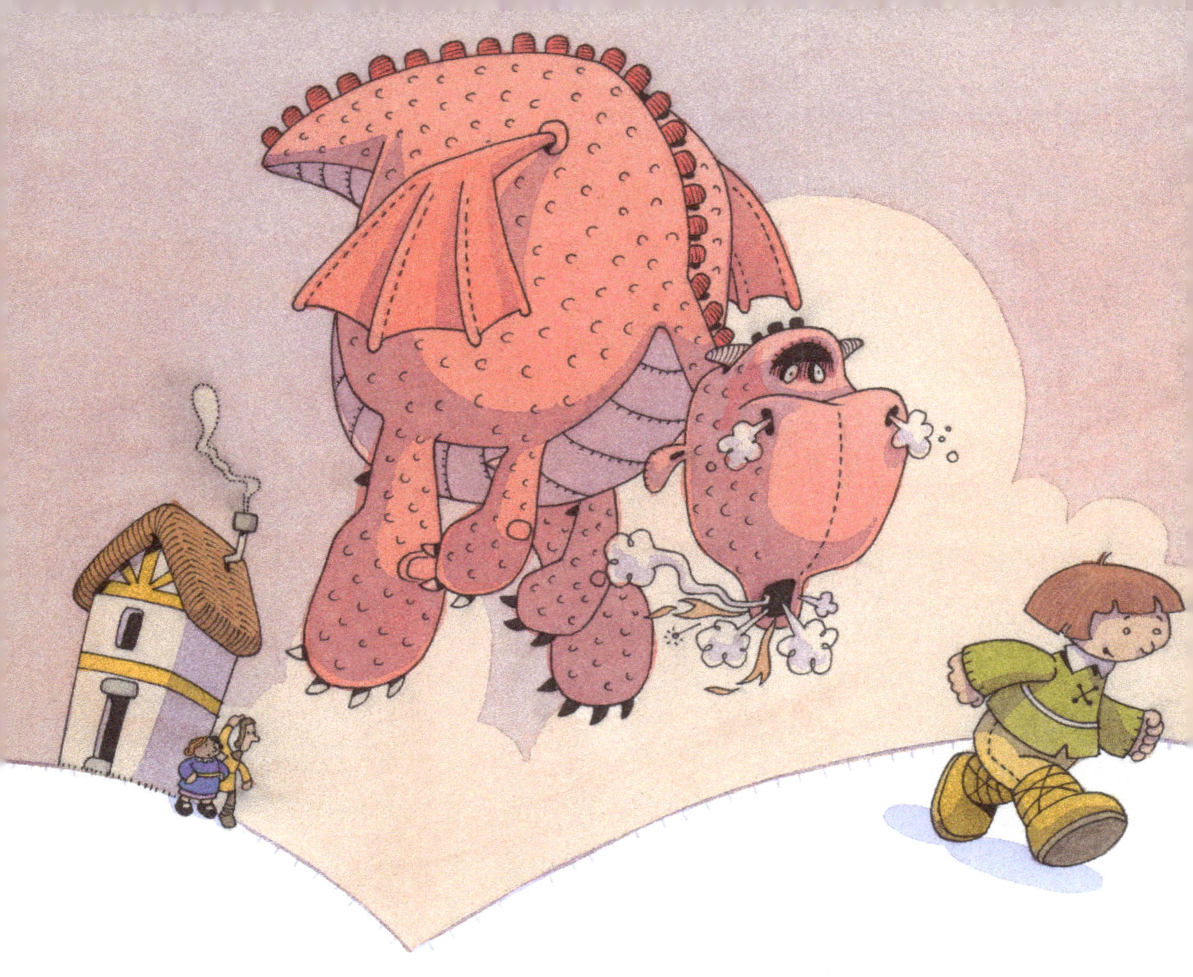

No!

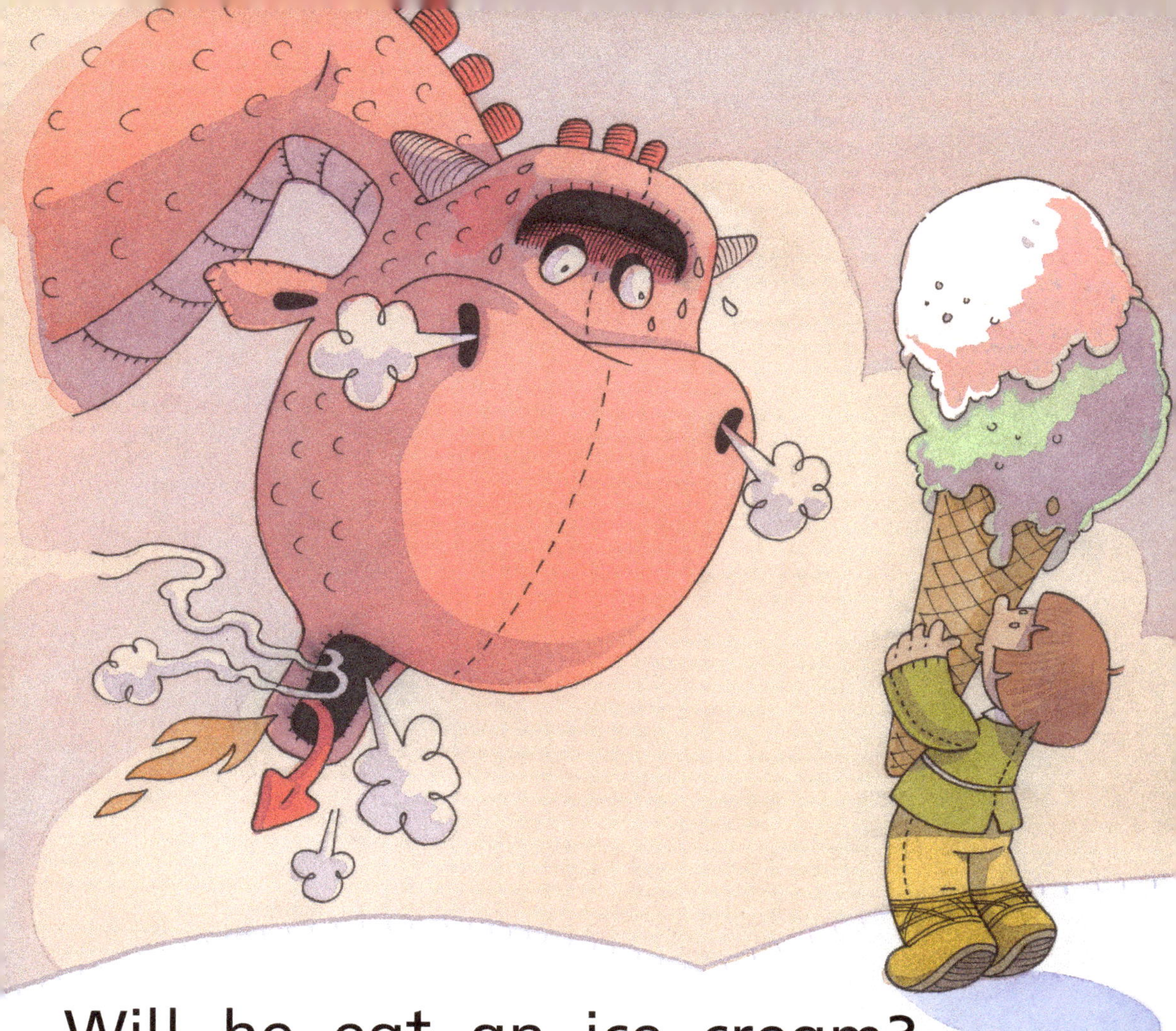

Will he eat an ice cream?

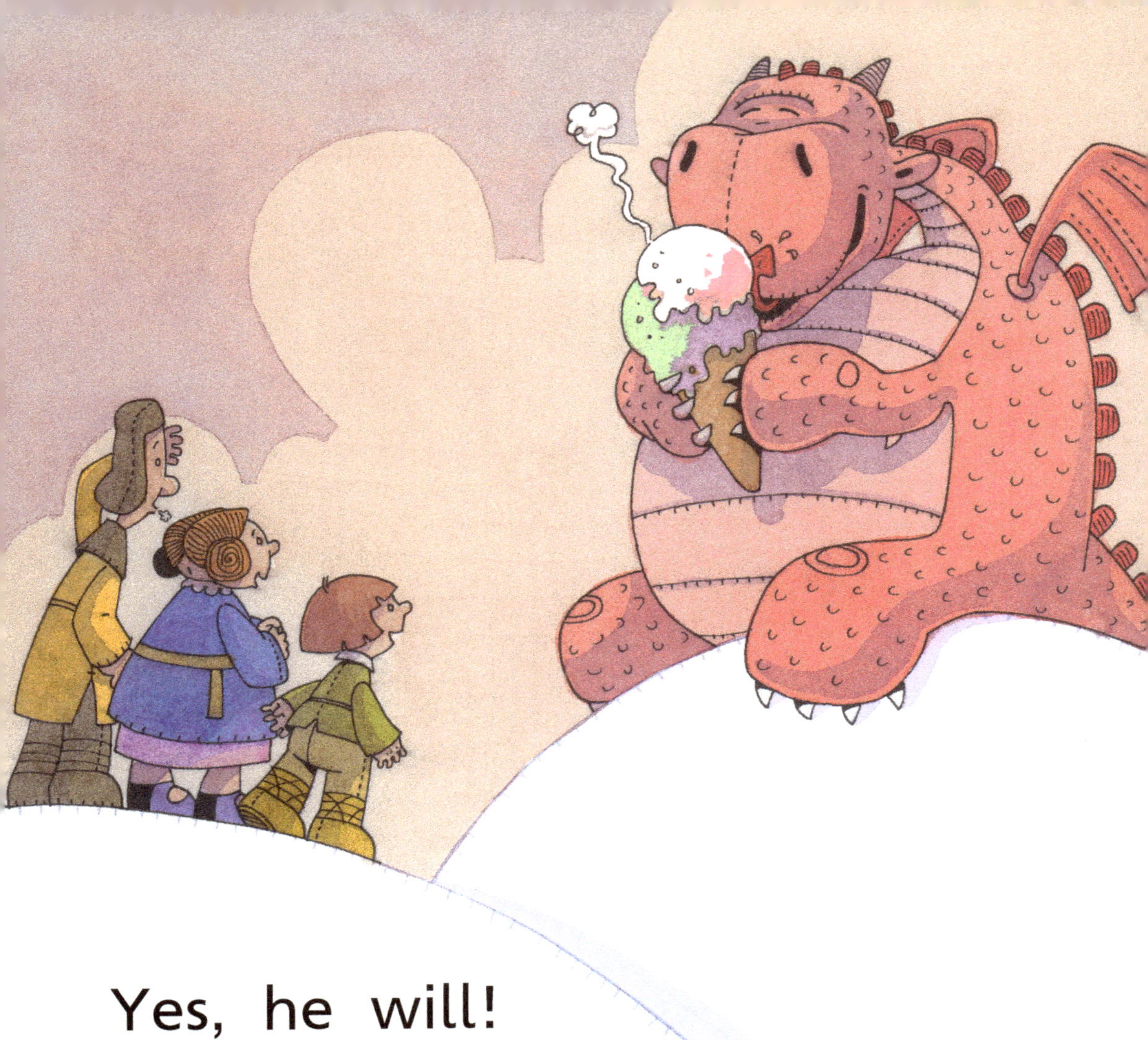

Yes, he will!